A Let's-Read-and-Find-Out Book™

DANGER—ICEBERGS!

by Roma Gans illustrated by Richard Rosenblum

REVISED EDITION

A Harper Trophy Book
Harper & Row, Publishers

The *Let's-Read-and-Find-Out Book*™ series was originated by Dr. Franklyn M. Branley, Astronomer Emeritus and former Chairman of the American Museum–Hayden Planetarium, and was formerly co-edited by him and Dr. Roma Gans, Professor Emeritus of Childhood Education, Teachers College, Columbia University. Text and illustrations for each of the more than 100 books in the series are checked for accuracy by an expert in the relevant field. The titles available in paperback are listed below. Look for them at your local bookstore or library.

Air Is All Around You
A Baby Starts to Grow
The BASIC Book
Bees and Beelines
Bits and Bytes
Comets
Corn Is Maize
Danger—Icebergs!
Digging Up Dinosaurs
Dinosaurs Are Different
A Drop of Blood
Ducks Don't Get Wet
Fireflies in the Night
Flash, Crash, Rumble, and Roll
Fossils Tell of Long Ago
Germs Make Me Sick!
Gravity Is a Mystery

Hear Your Heart
How a Seed Grows
How Many Teeth?
How to Talk to Your Computer
Hurricane Watch
Is There Life in Outer Space?
Look at Your Eyes
Me and My Family Tree
Meet the Computer
The Moon Seems to Change
My Five Senses
My Visit to the Dinosaurs
No Measles, No Mumps for Me
Oxygen Keeps You Alive
The Planets in Our Solar System
Rock Collecting
Rockets and Satellites

The Skeleton Inside You
The Sky Is Full of Stars
Snow Is Falling
Straight Hair, Curly Hair
Sunshine Makes the Seasons
A Tree Is a Plant
Turtle Talk
Volcanoes
Water for Dinosaurs and You
What Happens to a Hamburger
What I Like About Toads
What Makes Day and Night
What the Moon Is Like
Why Frogs Are Wet
Wild and Woolly Mammoths
Your Skin and Mine

Library of Congress Cataloging-in-Publication Data
Gans, Roma, 1894–
    Danger—icebergs!

    (A Let's read-and-find-out science book)
    Rev. ed. of: Icebergs. 1964.
    Summary: Explains how icebergs are formed from
glaciers, move into the ocean, create hazards to ships,
and melt away.
    1. Icebergs—Juvenile literature. [1. Icebergs]
I. Rosenblum, Richard, ill. II. Gans, Roma, 1894–
III. Title. IV. Series.
GB2403.8.G35 1987   551.3'42   87-531
ISBN 0-690-04627-8
ISBN 0-690-04629-4 (lib. bdg.)

    (A Let's read-and-find-out book)
    "A Harper Trophy Book."
ISBN 0-06-445066-X (pbk.)   87-45143

Arctic
Ocean

North Pole

ASIA
SIBERIA

GREENLAND

ALASKA

Baffin Bay

CANADA

ENGLAND

EUROPE

NORTH
AMERICA

U·S·A

Pacific
Ocean

Atlantic
Ocean

AFRICA

EQUATOR

SOUTH
AMERICA

N

WHERE
ICEBERGS FORM

ANTARCTICA
South Pole

Year after year, snow falls in the North. It falls on Alaska, Canada, Siberia, and Greenland. It also falls on the South Pole in Antarctica—where the penguins are.

Even the summer is cold in those places, so the snow does not melt. Over thousands of years it gets packed harder and harder until it is ice. In some places the ice can be three miles deep. This big cover of ice is called a glacier.

GREENLAND (BAFFIN BAY)

As the ice gets thicker and thicker in the glacier, it pushes toward the ocean.

The ocean waves beat hard against it. They make deep cracks in the glacier. All at once, there is a loud roar as a chunk of the glacier breaks off. This great chunk of ice is an iceberg.

Thousands of icebergs break off from glaciers each year. Some are large and look like shiny mountains. Others look like big buildings. Some are very wide and flat. Entire towns could be built on them.

Bergs float away from the glacier slowly, moving only three or four miles per hour. You can walk faster than many bergs float. Ocean currents sweep them in and out of a straight line on their way to warmer waters. It may be three or four years before some bergs melt completely away.

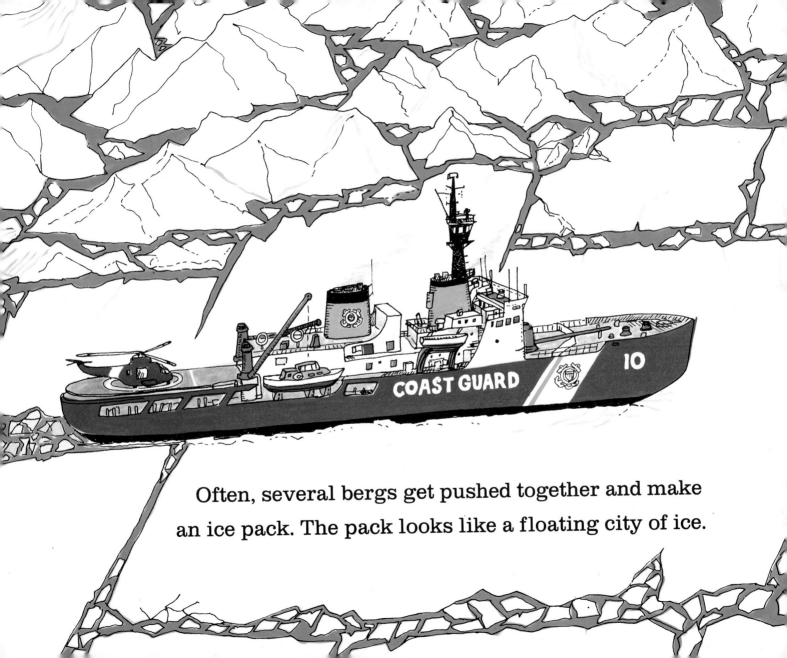

Often, several bergs get pushed together and make an ice pack. The pack looks like a floating city of ice.

Sometimes an iceberg tilts to one side. It may even turn upside down. If it touches bottom, its high peaks will be scraped away. Sometimes little bergs may break off a big berg.

Sailors can see only the tops of bergs. About one-eighth of a berg floats above water, and about seven-eighths is hidden below. The part below stretches out deep and wide; it often has sharp edges. Ships stay far away to be safe, even from small bergs.

Holes are made in icebergs when the ice melts or is gashed out as a berg scrapes land. Seals and polar bears often crawl into these holes. Seal pups have been born in iceberg hollows. You can hear their yelps and barks.

Bubbles of air form in an iceberg, and when they
break, anyone near hears a loud boom.

22

Hundreds of years ago there were brave sailors who crossed the Atlantic in wooden ships. They kept watch day and night. They had no telescopes or radios to guide them. They steered away from icebergs. Even when the sailors kept good watch, ships sometimes ran into icebergs and were sunk.

Even strong modern ships have struck bergs. One such crash happened in April 1912. A ship called the *Titanic* sailed from England on its first voyage. "Titanic" means large. The ship was the biggest and most beautiful ship ever built. No storms or icebergs could sink it—or so people said.

After four calm days of sailing, Captain E. J. Smith got radio messages that there were icebergs ahead. The ship sailed on.

Another radio alert came, but too late. There was a jerk and a grinding crash. The *Titanic* had hit an iceberg. Seams in the ship's metal hull began to give way.

At first, people were not scared. But as the water began to pour in, they knew they were in danger. Lifeboats were lowered. Everything was done to save lives, but more than 1,500 passengers and crew members drowned in the icy Atlantic.

The news of the disaster was carried around the world: "Iceberg Sinks *Titanic*."

The *Titanic* was about 500 miles from the North American coast. Many ships got its SOS signals. None could get there in time to help.

The berg that sank the *Titanic* was not large.
Survivors of the disaster said the berg's highest point
was about 100 feet above water. Below water it may
have extended 500 feet down. It was almost 1,000 feet
wide. The iceberg had broken off a glacier in
Greenland, on Baffin Bay. For three years it had

moved slowly south in the Atlantic with many much larger bergs.

After the sinking of the *Titanic*, the berg drifted on. As it moved into warmer waters, it began to melt. It became filled with holes, and pieces broke off. It got smaller and smaller. The last of the berg disappeared months after the tragedy.

New icebergs break off from glaciers each year. Thousands of icebergs still float in the oceans and seas where ships sail. But only this one berg has come to be called "The Iceberg."

Ships today have more than telescopes and radios to sight icebergs. They also have airplanes, radar, the coast guard, and satellites to alert them. Now those who sail the oceans see icebergs but feel safe.

The iceberg that drowned over 1,500 human beings—and destroyed three years of expert workmanship on the beautiful *Titanic*—caused the greatest sea disaster of all time. Even today, all who sail the oceans know they must steer clear of the power of icebergs.